Want to learn our number names?

Gusto ka makahibalo ngan sa mga numero?

It is very easy and a lot of fun!

Pirte ka sayon og lingaw!

Say-along our little jingle

Kanta uban kanamo!

ANG ISTORYA SANG MGA NUMERO

THE NUMBER STORY

SMALL BOOK ONE

ENGLISH - CEBUANO

*Numbers Teach Children
Their Number Names*

written and illustrated by

MISS ANNA

Early Reader Edition of *The Number Story 1*
Bronze Medal Winner, 2016 Wishing Shelf Book Award

Cover by | Lumpy Publishing
Layout by | Lumpy Publishing
Translated by Justin
Coloring by Jieeun Woo and Maria Mirabella

Library of Congress Control Number: 2018902040

Names: Miss Anna, author.
Title: Number story : numbers teach children their number names / Miss Anna.
Description: Portland, OR: Lumpy Publishing, 2018.
Identifiers: ISBN 978-1-945977-73-2 | LCCN 2018902040
Summary: The pictures and rhymes present stories which introduce numbers 0-10.
Subjects: LCSH Numeration—English--Cebuano--Pictorial works--Juvenile literature. | BISAC JUVENILE NONFICTION /
Languages: English--Cebuano
Classification: LCC QA141.3 .M57 2018 | DDC 513—dc23

Publisher: Lumpy Publishing
Website: www.missannabooks.com
Email: missanna@missannabooks.com

Paperback: ISBN 978-1-945977-73-2
Printed in the U.S.A.   1 3 5 7 9 10 8 6 4 2

starting from Number One!

Sugdan nato sa numero usa!

1

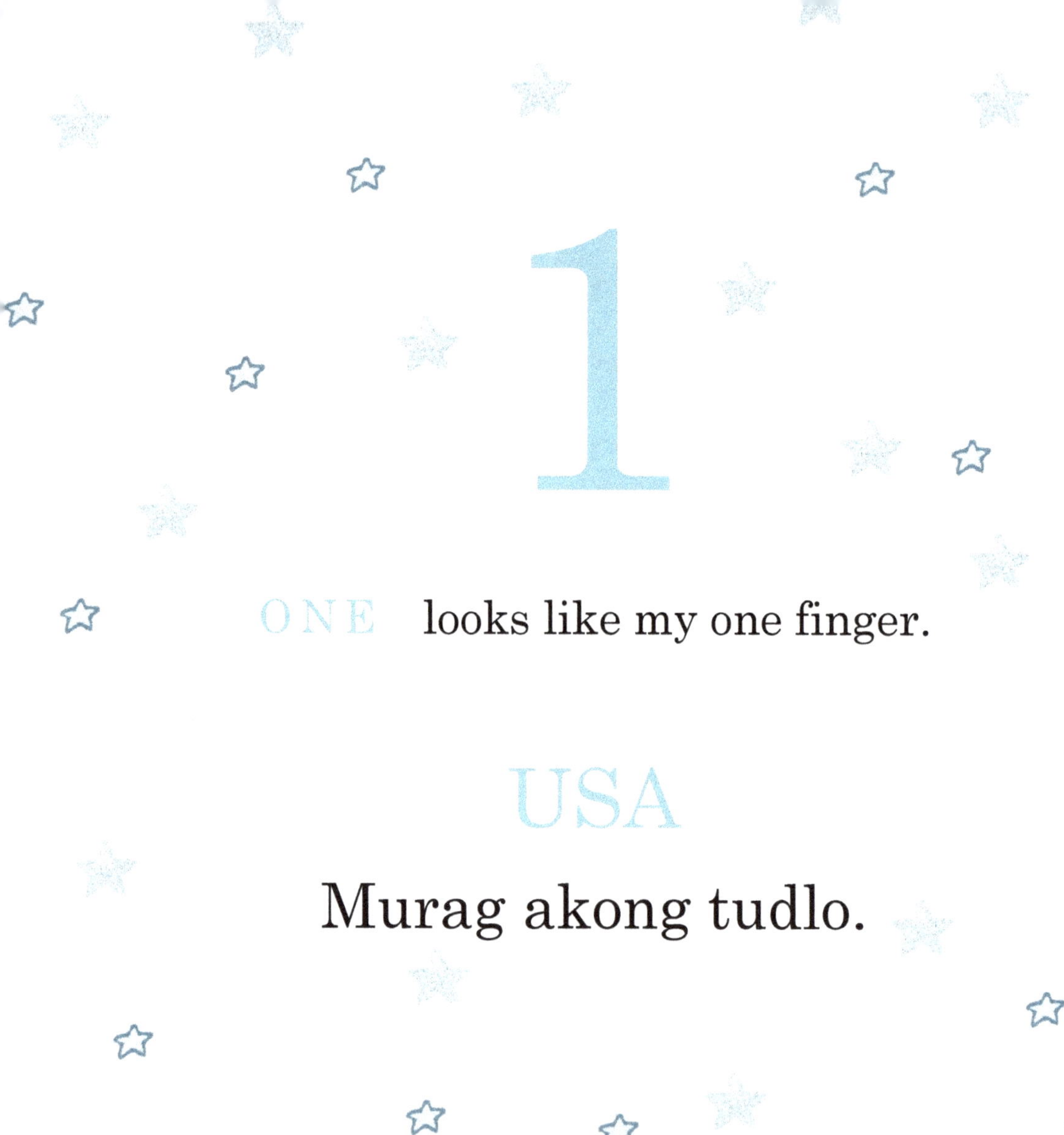

ONE looks like my one finger.

USA

Murag akong tudlo.

ONE!
USA!

2

TWO trails a tail.

DUA

Naa siyay ikog.

A TAIL! USA KA IKOG!

3

THREE has bumps.

TULO

Mura siyag buntod.

Tan-awa ang mga berde na buntod!

4

FOUR   carries a sail.

UPAT

Naa siyay layag.

4

A SAIL!

USA KA LAYAG!

5

FIVE is a racing track.

LIMA

ay dalan sa paglumba.

VROOM
BRUUUMM!
1

SIX curves like a snail.

UNOM

ay usa ka suso.

A SNAIL!   USA KA SUSO!

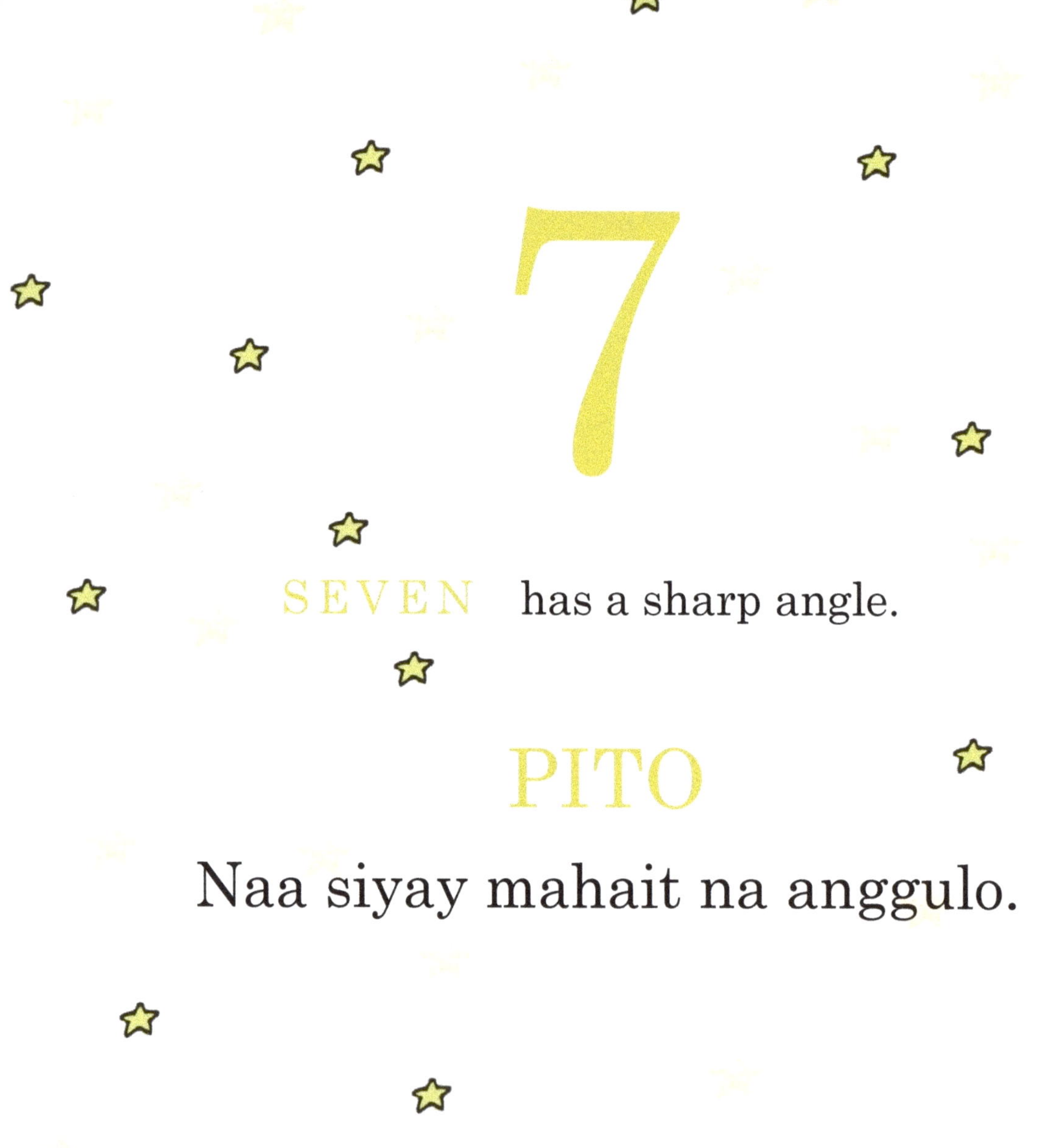

7

BE CAREFUL! IT'S SHARP!
PAG AMPING! MAHAIT!

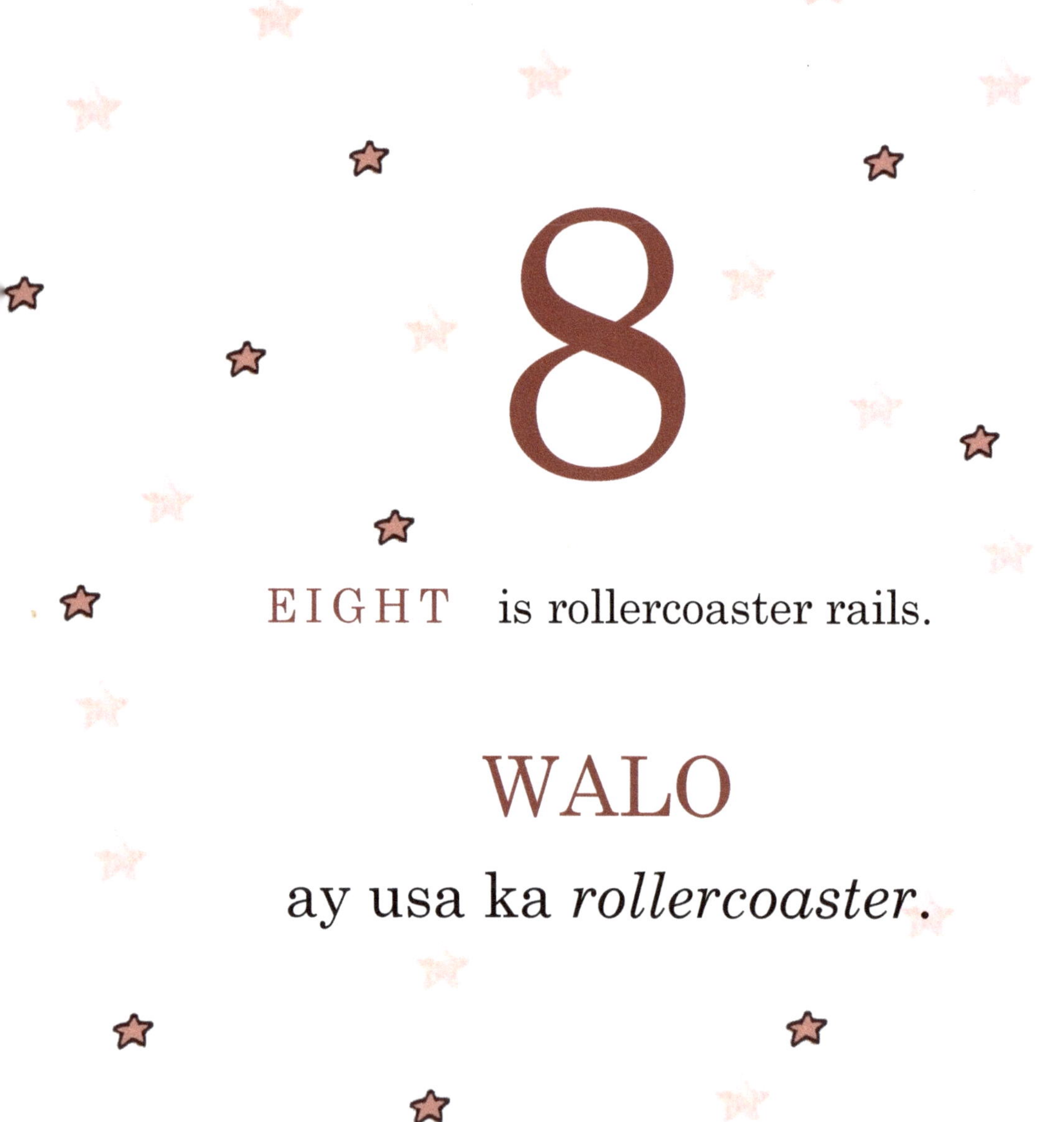

8

EIGHT is rollercoaster rails.

WALO

ay usa ka *rollercoaster*.

YiPPEE!
YIPPEE!

NINE is a bubble on a stick.

SIYAM

ay usa ka bula sa tugsok.

A BUBBLE! USA KA BULA!

10

TEN   is an eye of a whale.

PULO

ay usa ka mata sa balyena.

KIHAT!
WINK!

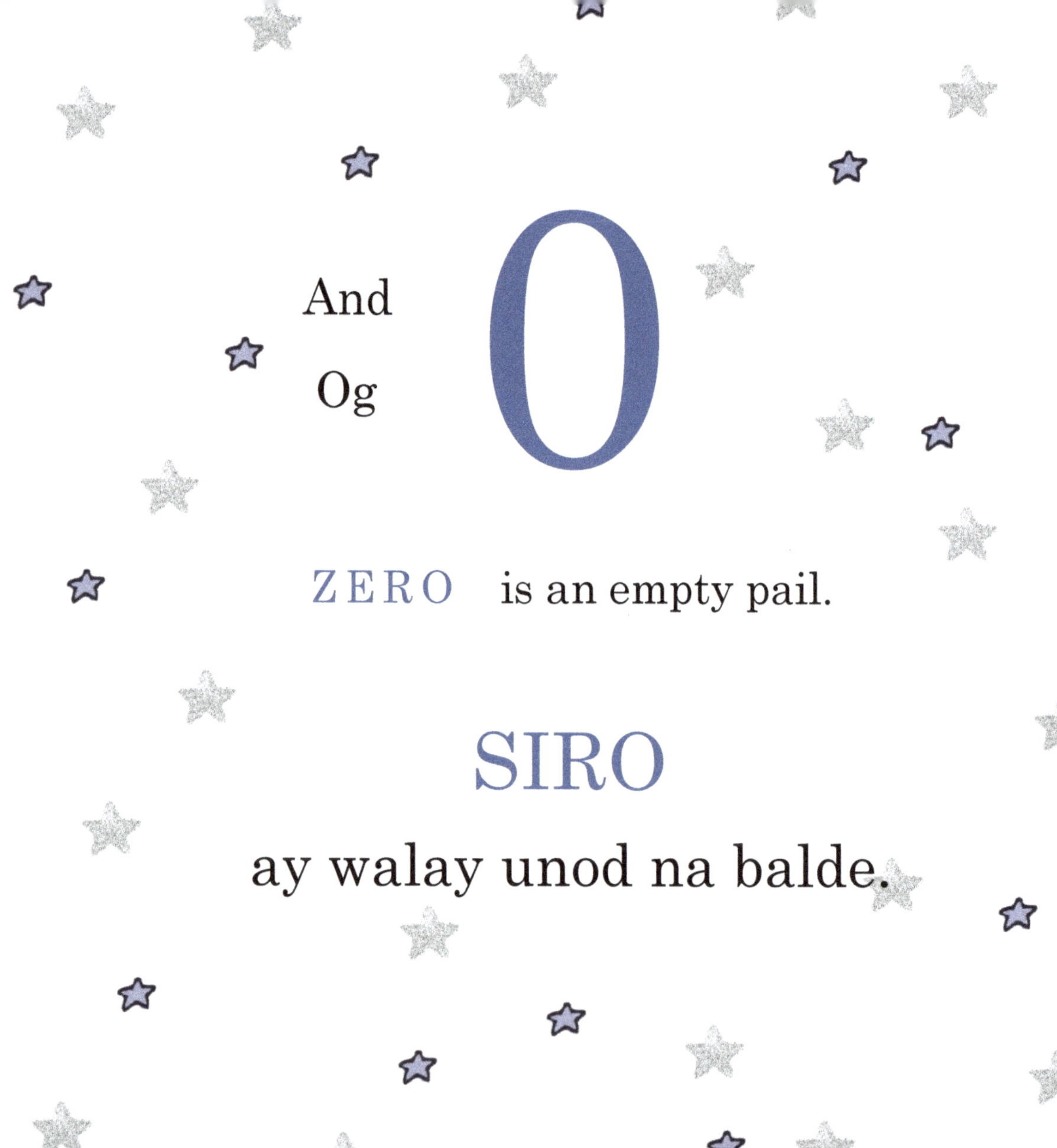

And
Og

O

ZERO   is an empty pail.

SIRO

ay walay unod na balde.

IT'S
EMPTY!
Walay unod!

Thank you for playing with us today.

We had a lot of fun too!

Salamat sa pag kanta kaning

kantaha uban sa amo-a.

Nalingaw pud mi kaayo!

We are your Number friends,
Zero to Ten,
Who will be here for you~
Kami imong mga amigo og amiga
Siro ngadto Pulo.
Pirme mi naa diri para kanimo ~

Bye-bye now!
See you again soon!
Bay-bay na sa karon!
Magkita napod ta sa sunod !

The Numbers are *SINGING* too!

To sing-a-long, look for Miss Anna Number Story
at your favorite music store like iTUNES.

MP3

Numbers 0-10
IDENTIFYING
& COUNTING

Numbers 11-20
& Ordinals
first, second, third...

Numbers 0-100
& Place Values
ones, tens, hundreds.

About Clocks
& Telling Time
hours, minutes, second

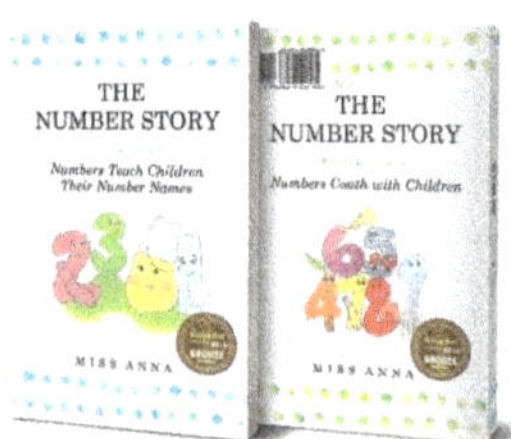

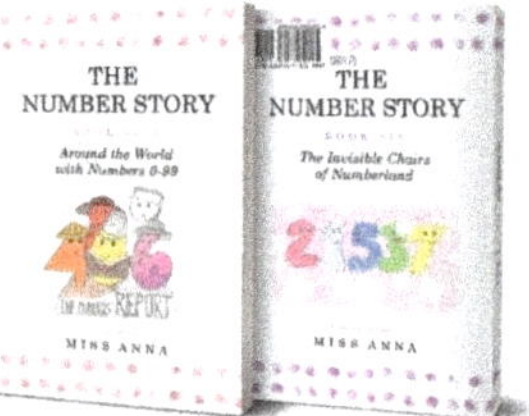

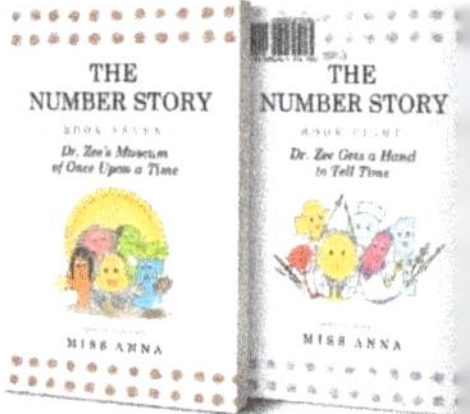

Number Story 1 & 2
isbn: 978-0-996216-48-7

Number Story 3 & 4
isbn: 978-1-945977-01-5

Number Story 5 & 6
isbn: 978-1-945977-06-0

Number Story 7 & 8
isbn: 978-1-949320-40-

For more Miss Anna books to love,
visit us at

www.missannabooks.com

Numbers are working hard all over the world!
Come Travel the World with Us!